Gallery Books
Editor: Peter Fallon

BOOTERSTOWN

Frank McGuinness

BOOTERSTOWN

Gallery Books

Booterstown
is first published
simultaneously in paperback
and in a clothbound edition
on 27 October 1994.

The Gallery Press
Loughcrew
Oldcastle
County Meath
Ireland

ISBN 1 85235 135 7 *(paperback)*
       1 85235 136 5 *(clothbound)*

The Gallery Press receives financial assistance from An Chomhairle
Ealaíon / The Arts Council, Ireland.

Contents

for my mother and father

The Palm of His Hand

for Sarah

My father knows the water like the palm of his hand.
He can read the sea as if it were his son.
When I look at his face, it is salt and storm.
The same face has looked for life at the Atlantic.
I sometimes think he has married the ocean.
This marriage has lasted longer than the earth.
Bigger than the earth, if the truth were told.
I have never looked at my father in the water.
Were I to do so, he would disown me.
This would crack my heart as a leaping stone cracks.
Such sorrow is possible, as the size of the sea is possible.
The size of sorrow is the size of my father.
He has never looked at the palm of his hand.

The Coral Beach by the Sea at Carraroe

for Kevin Barry

This is a planet, and there is water in the craters here.
A bloodsucker sleeps peacefully in the centre of this planet.
The place has only ever been disturbed by the first foot
That celebrates a new year, a new life on the coral beach
At the very edge of Connacht, where hell has no fury
But the *sean nós* of gulls who sing in lost tongues.
Two girls, Ruth and Rachel, beside the rabbinical sea
That heard the prayers of tribes long lost to America —
O weeping wall of sea — write the bible, their covenant
Of childhood in the pink sand.

                        It is tranquil today,
The sea at Carraroe. A tranquil day to spend together.
Should any ship appear to darken the horizon,
May they be ships that pass in the night, as if night
Were a phase we were all passing through,
So that by morning, faces washed, mouths cleaned,
The night seems clear as daylight, the night of lost desire,
The night a tranquil day to spend together
And to repeat, you promise, should the desire take us,
For through mist and cloud and music
Comes the sweep of still water, lake, land,
Green, purple, all there for the happy seeing,
Sky, contained, eternally in water.

                        And I have heard
The sea at Carraroe. It is condemned to speak
As follows; it says, this will pass, this day
We spend together will pass, all is ebb and flow,
But let it pass, let it, never mind.
The mind is your loved illusion.
Love what is illusion.

It would be great to believe
The sea at Carraroe. I wish I could hear it
Hold its breath and make a wish come true
As Ruth and Rachel wish the coral turn to comb
And the sea to sugar to stiffen their long hair,
So they could dance the bible in the hope
Of human happiness.

I am sorry. This cannot happen.
All that can is to hear the ocean weeping
It cannot turn to rock. It should change its tune,
Indeed it really should, but it is going to America,
And like a lost tribe beats its head against the wall
Of pink coral of the beach at Carraroe.
That is why the coral's broken, or so I am told.

Booterstown

in memory of Gregory Lysaght

1

Beneath my house a smugglers' tunnel carves
Its way from a cave that looks into the Irish Sea
And ends outside the Catholic Church in Booterstown.
Was it there I heard, as a student, a drunk priest
Sermonize in screams against Friedrich Nietzsche
And defy the death of God? Is Death a smuggler
And God the precious object that the citizens
Of Death's own country coveted above all worldly goods?
I can believe in a dying country, in the citizens
Who are God-fearing and who have tempers that rise
Like high tide to break and furrow the rocky walls
Of the white railway station at Booterstown:
There the birds scream like mad priests
And the sea is offering its consecrated wines.
I can believe the birds in Booterstown Sanctuary
Finding their way to this house through the tunnel,
Deserting the fresh air, preferring to breed underground.
This is what they did on the day of a death,
A young man whose heart stopped in its second decade,
Whom we called Gregory. The neighbourhood mourned.
I saw the women's hair grow long in mourning
In this avenue of holy places and sacred names,
For sacred be the willows of Willow Place that weep
For Gregory. Go search through McCabe Villas,
St Helens Road, can you find him in Cross Avenue?
These are the places of his childhood, children hide.
Ah, you have found him in the Catholic Church,
His body laid out, his sister weeping,
As a donkey in the field outside starts to bray.

They played there, a boy and girl, discovering
The wheel. It is the wheel of fortune.
The wheel of fortune turns for good and ill.

2

In the living-room where I write, Gregory,
Above the mess of books and papers on the table,
There hangs a painting. It is red and orange
And gold and black. It is a flower on fire.
It is light itself. Do you remember light?
The light you would love is a gold medal
Picked up at the Olympics or at Wembley.
I would turn all of Booterstown Avenue
Into a football pitch, kick the fearless ball
With pleasure, break all the respectable windows.
Or you could sprint to win — I estimate the distance
To be covered in ten seconds as that between
The Punch Bowl and the Nook. I can see you
Race it in ten seconds. Blink and you'd miss it.
Like a flower's life. Blink and you miss it.
Do you remember flowers? Do you remember life?
Has it turned into a wax museum? History?
Wax moulds and melts, breaks and is found
In the ears of the living to block the sound
Of birds singing in the Booterstown trees
On the autumn morning of your death.
We wash the dead, we wash our ears and hear
What it is the birds sing about your life.
They remember you, one Saturday, in your mother's
Post office, working, and a gang attacked you,
Pulling a gun, wanting money. You gave it,
Knowing that money should give way to the gun
For it is only money, and life is more lovely

Than the gun and the gang. Well done, well done.
Gregory, that day you defied death.
You praised this life. But the good die young,
The rest of us reside in Booterstown Avenue,
Hostages to fortune in Booterstown Avenue,
Living where we live in Booterstown Avenue.

Sister Anne Breslin

These days I move between sleep and dream.
Dreaming is easier on the bones.
I swim through my sleep to a strange rock.
The rock's in the ocean, the ocean's in my bones.

I am turning into wind, into pink water.
Wind and water took a vow of silence.
I rock in the bed between sleep and dream,
Trying to remember when there was silence.

Noise is a word away from nuisance.
I am a nuisance but I once was water.
I wore down my fingers to the touch of stone
And built my house from the self-same rock.
Fingers to stone, noise to nuisance —
Dreaming is easier on the bones.

Joe Chadwick, Koli Koli Pass, Hawaii, 8 April 1992

1

The peaceful April today.
Hawaii is sea.
Long forgotten, the Japanese

Flying through Koli Koli Pass,
War in Pearl Harbour,
The sea a broken necklace

Round a woman's throat,
Hands bombard her, child
Looking for attention.

You know I dislike attention.
Sit with you
Alone in lovely valleys

Where the sea whispers
Like a shell through us
Its terrible secrets to the sky.

It knows what they've shared.
I'm a peaceful man
But I enjoy the war

Between the sky and the sea.
They are blue in the face arguing
Over which is more important.

Neither is important.
What is important
Is that they are both terrible

In their whispers of eternity.
I dislike eternity.
It has no memory, it forgets everything.

2

A year I spent in Dublin, writing on Yeats,
Whom did I meet but the man himself, ghosting his life
Through the suburbs of Sandymount and Ballsbridge
Where he first witnessed the light of day and where
I was wandering. A hazel wand in the air.
He nodded to the air, I replied, and asking
If I were interested in the Orient, he suggested
We might investigate the Chester Beatty Library,
Given to the Irish nation years after his death.
I was reared to respect the dead and agreed.

We walked in step down Shrewsbury Road,
Me imagining who might live in these big houses,
Yeats keeping his imaginings to himself,
When, out of the blue, he produced a Chinese snuff box,
The painting of a red kite flying on its inside,
And placed it in my warm hand, the box cold as bone,
So I could examine the delicate empty vessel
Which I did, warming it with my hand,
And I remarked how carelessly the kite flew
In the air of the empty box. This pleased him.

There is no admission charge to the Chester Beatty.
The day we entered Calligraphy was closed.
Yeats had disappeared by this stage of my journey.
I believe he may have vanished into the jade book
Unfolded for an Emperor seeking eternity in words
Reading from back to front, cheating the linear,

As Yeats would have approved, hence his disappearance.
I registered my loss by looking at the book
Until my eyes had turned to jade and tears
Were neither possible nor indeed desirable.

Who would weep for a ghost but the ghost himself?
Who can hear a ghost weeping but the living left behind?
Such thoughts I will pack away in a black dowry box
Of Japanese lacquer where they placed the tale of all their days
And then I will reject sorrow's offer of marriage
And propose instead to the gorgeous silk robe
Where the dragon resides, its intricated flesh
The golden threads that lead us to the place we began
In the womb of the sun, the loins of the moon,
In the baited breath of the beating heart.

Today I hear my heart in the Chester Beatty,
My breath in my body, the museum of my days
And nights, crumbling the papyrus — a Gospel of St John —
Ending in apocalypse, if I should let it.
No. Let my life be an act of revelation,
An instrument to weigh the heart light as a feather
Having loved and done itself justice. Justice . . .
I am a man contemplating the life to come,
A stranger seeing ghosts in Dublin. The end
Will be as calm as the cold bone in my hand.

3

Empty my ash from a beautiful boat
Into delicate, masculine water.
In the end it was easy to go into the fire.

The boat in the water belonged to a pirate,
The flag it flies is skull and crossbones.
In the end it is easy to go into the water.

Remember me swimming in the ocean,
Beloved of water, fearless of fire.

Ho Chi Minh Park

When it made the front page of the *Belfast Telegraph*
We knew we had a scandal on our hands.
Who could ever forget Ho Chi Minh Park? Laugh

If you must that a small Catholic town,
Stuck somewhere out of sight, out of mind,
Was to be given for the lost and the found

A municipal park bearing that Communist name.
The man who owned the land demanded it so.
Could it come to pass that Ho Chi Minh's reign

Would, through Council Compulsory Purchase,
Be celebrated by the ebb and flow
Of the sweet Atlantic bringing breeze and haze

To the self-same town, touching the green field
Of the self-same man? Would this happen to us?
Being young, being careful, I yielded

To wisdom. Why not John F Kennedy Park?
Pope John XXIII? Take a bus
To Derry if you want to enter the dark.

Fourteen miles away Derry reeled like a nun
Who's hit the bottle after fifty years
Of deprivation. And we who were sons

And daughters of revolution laughed
In South Vietnam at Ho Chi Minh. Fear,
I suppose, till the *Belfast Telegraph*

Published and bedamned the red menace scare.
It never happened, Ho Chi Minh Park, we didn't dare,
But someone kept the newspaper somewhere.

The Milk Town

Who has ever crossed the threshold of Maggie Platt's cottage,
An empty can of buttermilk in his yellow hand,
Waiting for it to be filled from a sour bowl,
And come Friday faced walking the Hill Head again?

I say it's not possible to sleigh the Hill Head,
Charge up the Pound Lane right to the Royal Bank,
Getting no push or shove from any hand,
I say there's never been such a slide.

Who now remembers the Burns that brought the milk
Locking up their bicycles in the abandoned forge,
Going to the pictures in St Mary's Hall,
Milk like mercury spilt solid on their hands?

Did anyone dander past Maggie Platt's cottage
Far away from home — the trees, the trees, the trees?
Did anyone get lost in the green of shadows
Where the Mill River was starting to wind?

Wind like a rope, this winding river,
Hanging by the neck of the crying town.
Why is it crying? Ask the one for hours
Seen standing on Looking Glass Brae,

Wondering the reason for living in the Milk Town,
Miles from the pictures, the shop and the shore,
Happy as Larry looking at the Hill Head
In houses that shone from the sun and the stars.

Open House

The rooms we live in number four.
Too small to throw big parties.
Friends think we'll separate.

> I feel your body and mine
> Still meet in time at night,
> Not just when you're restless.
> Then coffee in bed;
> Prolonged last fag.
> My spider in the bath,
> Save me.
> Laugh, I'll leave you aching.

Two runaway trains,
Going over the hill,
Rusting to a halt?
Should we leave the tracks?

> Perfect coupling demands imitation,
> I couldn't be like you.
> Never. You hate my silences.

Is five years saying something?
Taking each other on
Still excites like venial sin,
And I'm glad we're mortal.
So welcome morning warmly.
A good, long lie-in.
Breakfast's on me.

> The laziest man you know.
> I've kept you awake talking.
> Unfair, you know it well.
> If you want to think that, do.

I cannot stand your —
No, let today be tender.
We've letters to answer.
You write, I'll sign my name.

The Torn Sleeves

My lover of horses is half-awake.
Tonight I would ride him home to Peterborough.
Tear his white skin tooth and claw. Make
What you will.

        So.

We are silk.

My lover of horses knows his own mind.
I feed him coffee and sugar and oh
He is half-starved of my caress. Find
What you will.

        So.

My lover of horses loves me to death.
Death is a game of touch and go.
I know the way my lover knows. Breathe
What you will.

        So.

We are sleeves.

Lullaby

for Christopher Morash

The man in the moon
Looked into your eyes

Sleep sleep sleep child

The birds of the air
Came from Paradise

Sleep sleep sleep child

The man in the moon
looks into your eyes

Sleep sleep sleep child

Prospero's Daughter

for Marianne and Eva

When I put my hands in cold water
I remember my mother.
One day we went travelling
In a boat that women wove.
We were sailing to an island
Whose name the sea forgot.
She had her books and charms
Hidden up her sleeve.
The elements were merciful,
Unravelling the knots
That bind mother and daughter,
Mother and daughter, mother and daughter . . . .

I asked the wind who my mother was.
He sighed, you have broken laws
The day you went travelling
In a boat that no man sailed.
We were banished from a country
Whose name the sea forgot.
I had our bread and milk
Hidden in my veil.
The elements were merciful,
Unravelling the knots
That bind mother and daughter,
Mother and daughter, mother and daughter . . . .

When I put my hands in cold water
I remember my mother,
The day we went travelling
In a boat that women wove.

I heard her heart breaking,
Stitched it to my sleeve.
I heard her heart beating,
Stitched it to my sleeve.
O elements, be merciful,
Unravelling the knots
That bind mother and daughter,
Mother and daughter, mother and daughter . . . .

The Baker Takes a Walk

for Anne

A white man goes for a walk at night,
Beneath a bare tree, his body like a branch
Falling, as if it were a bird, learning to sing,
To fly, forgetting the earth is a black place.
A bird, a branch, the man walks sideways
To his place of destination, smelling bread
In the air, as if it were flowering, the air
That is, but all that he is is the man in white,
The smell of him disturbing the night
That wears black velvet.

                    And so he walks,
For eternity, walking as if the field
He crosses were Everest — he'll never make it.
Nor does he wish to cease walking,
For all the baker wishes is to smell bread,
Since bread is his touch, his taste,
His be all and end all, hence he wears white,
For his body is flour and water, and the night
And tree his yeast.

                    He rises. It is predictable.
What is he thinking of, the baker
Going for a walk? Is that predictable?
I think he imagines tonight he will bake
The perfect bread, bread to feed five thousand,
Bread to last forever, bread to build a house from,
Bread where people share their wine and eggs,
A perfect breaking, a perfect pouring,
And bread, let him bake bread forever.

                              The baker —
He knows nothing of these intentions, being simply
A working man, caught forever in the act
Of walking, the art of baking, saving the salt of his tears
For the job in hand, knowing salt
Will be a necessary ingredient to spice
The life that requires bread and bakers.
This night the white he wears is a Chinese
Symbol of the dead. He is Asian.
He is in exile. He is in Europe.
We eat bread, in Europe, and in Asia. He bakes it.

David Hockney

for Vivienne

Truth, stranger than a dolmen's
sign, is best left undeciphered;
you grasp it in water,
the blueness of its feathers,
trapped in pool-shaped cages,
unfree yet changing form.

And time also eludes precise
definition, unfinished
like parents caught
with features mirrored
beside remembered furniture
our bodies take weight from.

Elephant's hollowed foot-
stand, filled with umbrellas;
a jungle in the hallway,
savannah on the carpet.
Incongruously usual,
your house of hieroglyphics.

A shirt across the chair
awaits the bestower
to load the coloured shapes
that ricochet like bullets.
Magic is the tale
narrating objects' wonder.

To know we must leave home
and learn that word means fear,
let down our dampened hair
to raise the waiting kiss,
place yourself in light
illuminating darkness.

A Prayer to Saint Derek

Quite contrary is the garden where
Daffodils grow in autumn. This savage
February, who would raise their pretty
Heads above the ground? Yet last night,
Derek, the day after your dying, in
Maynooth College, great granite dome of
The Catholic Church, where I so much wanted you
To speak someday, there was a drag ball
In the Students' Union. Your Irish wake.

In this country it is done to celebrate
The dead. To bake bread in the oven
Of their memory. Drink the wine of their
Days and holy nights. Fuck them
With perfumed memory. Profound Englishman,
My generation's William Blake, my
Visionary, you would have smiled at our
Simplicity and sought the Anglican Church,
Strange within the grounds of Rome's seminary.

I would have misdirected you with pleasure,
My beautiful Brit. I would lead you to
The temple of a faithful friend. There you
Would toast with us in Carton Estate
The pride and joy of your eyes. Indian
Widows of the Raj would shell you
In purdah. And there, docile as a nun,
You would let your virginal ears roast
By sensual fire. Music is dangerous

Sex. This night, hear music in heaven.
Hear the music of the sphere that spins,
The sphere that is yourself, Derek Jarman,
Yourself alone — ourself alone, Ireland
Divided, England asleep. Our warring

Generations. Good Merlin, were you to bestow
One wish on these dying nations,
Let it be the beautiful lie, the lie
Of peace that passes all understanding.

I do not understand your dying
Too soon. I am not at peace with
Your passing. I want to greet you
In the precincts of the gorgeous square
At the heart of the old campus in Maynooth
College and explain why I work among
The faithful. Twice we nearly met,
Twice denied. Let me not deny you
The third time. In this square den,

This day of snow and bitter cold —
How God loves you, he is white as a ghost
With shock at your death, he sheds
Feathers — let us meet. Let me enter
The staff canteen with you and eat.
The roast beef of England, potatoes
From Ireland, spring onions. Let me peel
The onion of your art. Martyr, king,
Painter, hero, gardener, good philosopher:

Derek Jarman. Set Juno arguing with
Jupiter. Great dark Ganymede, turn
Into an eagle. Evaporate like snow.
This week there are men and women lost
In mountains. Save them. And lead us
Into protection. Show us where you see
The signs of the living. Where there's breath,
Let it be from your mouth, your last wish;
Heal us, free us. Let these things pass.

Four Ways to See Your Lover in Venice

1 Bellini

In all Venice you are the most handsome man.
I have come to that conclusion. At night
We lie in our grand double bed, our limbs
Bellini's madonna and child together. My love,
I am your transfiguration. Our prophets —
Their words like white sheets — dissolve to water,
And this eejit, my lover, leaps to spread
Panic in case anyone finds evidence. Tell them
A spreadeagled pose makes cocksucking
Easy. I like you like this, arms like
The quarter of a muscular clock, near
Striking, ready for attack. You wouldn't.
Love is without violence. You rise
From the deep. You are in love with water.

2 Veronese

Say I threw a last supper for yourself,
With friends, to share your birthday,
Would I do as you would ask me?
Take sufficient food and drink, excess it,
If there be flowers, have them everywhere,
And if there's music, play it low. Please.
You'll settle half by sterling cheque.
Invite no one that night who intends to sit alone.
Would I put you in the centre of the evening,
Taking stock of our friends and enemies?
Enemies on such a night? Yes, enemies.
There is a reason for every evil
In each human being. I wish I believed that,
Breaking bread, attending, wounding, watching.

3 *Titian*

I'll find you by Titian's grave.
At the high altar Our Lady ascends.
She has given up on life. It's death,
But it's miraculous. We'll bid farewell
To this place, and to Titian's grave,
And think of the letting go after love,
And think of loss, the going home,
Departures at the airport, at the train,
To go back to work. That's the way.
You'll travel alone in the smoking carriage,
Lighting up a purple Silk Cut, purple
Like the Virgin's shroud. Titian knew
That death is a matter of letting go,
A losing, a lighting up, a darkening.

4 Carpaccio

The root of light is water. Carpaccio
Told you that when you slayed the dragon.
Look the fire straight in the eyes and fear not
The Venetian gentleman, for he comes to
Lovers who are lost in the Orient of spices,
Strange as the smell of silk, trailing the way
From Europe in the wake of Marco Polo.
Then throw open the window of palaces and
Remember in the holy, silver water of
The heavenly canal the names of friends
Who travelled eastward to the rising sun,
Friends who're dead now, dead and buried,
They who were young, who were beautiful as
Carpaccio's name. And slay the dragon.

Patroclus

He was searching through the streets of Dublin,
Having chanced upon a boy glimpsed in the glass
Of the speeding DART on its way from Bray to Howth,
And he looked into the sleeping eyes of beauty,
Wishing he could waken the boy, in case he,
The boy, missed his destination, but disembarking
At Pearse Street Station, he had to let him sleep.

And then one winter evening in the Diamond, in Derry,
Frozen, wondering if the Union Jack floating
Over Walker's Monument would ever be hauled
From the mast, he caught sight of a blond Brit
Looking back at him, his short hair too short,
And imagined the hairlessness of his body
And wished that love were a language they could speak.

This was nothing compared to the man in Blackrock,
The Roccia Nera restaurant, and the reaction
To the golden ring on his long finger, the jacket linen,
The scent of his shirt, green and yellow check,
Listening to his body laughing, the dip of his fork
Into green pasta and yellow peppers —
He would have killed for him on the spot.

And what about in Galway, the Quays bar,
Where it was as if Caravaggio's model
For St John the Baptist in the Villa Borgese
Was sitting drinking a pint of Guinness —
Who nearly lost his brain and fell at his feet?
He kept his head and caught the Dublin train
And the whole of Connacht passed in dream.

In such a dream did Achilles see
How he looked at Patroclus
To shield him from all the eyes of Troy

And showed to him the wounds of war
That formed the secrets of his life.
Then baring heel and fearing death,
He let Patroclus touch him.

The Blindfolded Man

for Bosco and Lesley Hogan

I sit in a house in Rathgar, my mind
Obsessed by magic. I do not believe in
Rituals, but the eating of a meal
Requires manners. Manners maketh magic.

Somewhere in the mind's remotest quarters
There stirs a sense of being here before,
And straying into somewhere familiar,
I shoot my mouth off. Words are peculiar.

I see that room with perspicacity.
I see its ritual of furniture.
We sit, we talk, we eat and sing.

Not bad for a blindfolded man,
His cigarette the firing squad's magic.
This night we do not die.

Shavings

In Buncrana the bakery gave out
Shavings, strips of cooked apple,
Sugar and pastry. Lynch's bakery.

When word got out, you didn't shout
That there was sweetness going free. Hell
To pay if you blabbed. Nobody say

Nothing. These are for us, boys.
Years after, beside my man in bed,
I think about that secret sweetness.

Sometimes I wonder how to give him joy.
How to listen, how to have him fed
With fantasy, bringing him to lovely rest.

I'd like to fuck him in Plato's cave,
Our shadows souls we cannot save.
My lover likes his body shaved.

The Irish Sea

There are nights what lies between us
Is the Irish Sea.
Me not able to sleep a wink,
You dancing in your sleep.

My enemy, my England.

Who do you dance with as you sleep?
Handsome men you have loved?
I've met a few, they're not handsome,
Not to me at any rate.

My enemy, my England.

I am jealous of you sleeping,
Of the days I've never seen,
Jealous of the men who saw you
Naked dancing in your sleep.

There are nights I think of leaving
You to stew in your sleep
With the men who loved and lost you,
Sweetened night, and then were gone.

Fifteen years of love and loathing,
What the hell is that to you?
Tonight you are distant, as
Sky who turns the sea to blue.

My England, my enemy.

There are nights what lies between us
Is the Irish Sea.
Me not able to sleep a wink,
You dance naked in your sleep.

My England, my enemy,
I am the Irish Sea.

Across the Border

Say a girl and a boy go to a dance,
Say they stop behind for a bit of a chat,
I'd like to know what is the chance
That years after the dance, forgetting the band,
That chat might lead to an unmarked grave,
As her face, her feet, her hair, her hands,
The temple of her holy ghost — O salve
Regina — is violated by a bullet
Or the rough kiss of rope
He kept like a letter in his wallet
In case someday he'd to abandon hope
And sell his soul to the devil who says,
Betray the girl, betray the cause,
There are always means, there are always ways,
For remember: Keep thou holy the border's laws.

Across the border that's how they do things.
Do things to each other, women and men.
Take it for granted they do not swing,
But across the border anything can happen.

Green

in memory of Petra Kelly

I think the sun is crying,
The earth shines in its eyes.

I hear the sea being quiet.
The continent's on fire.

I think the sea is crying,
The earth and sun and fire.

The Wyf of Bath Returns to Flanders

for Catherine Bunyan

At the age of 700 I should mind my manners,
But since when did manners make a woman immortal?
I am the Wyf of Bath returned to Flanders,
And walking through Bruges, splendid in red stockings,
Attended by two gentlemen of an alien faith,
I'll throw pleasant shapes at what fancy my eye catches,
And my eye fancies what I keep my faith in.

The love of a good man might save me one day,
But who'd choose salvation when this sweet life,
Passing as slowly as a swan through the canals of Bruges,
The swan's neck like a lovely long white witch's hat,
This sweet neck — no, this sweet life, I meant,
Has brought me to Flanders for the first time in centuries,
So I must enjoy myself as if for the first time.

When Chaucer lit on me, he made me young, full of ragerye,
How kind to let me remember my youth,
So wild, so foolish, soft, crammed with memory —
Ah to hell with remembrance, to hell with happiness
If happiness be nothing more than a hand up the skirt
That went out of date with the ark —
I wasn't on the ark, they wouldn't let me in, so I swam.

It is hard to keep a good woman under.
What is a good woman, I asked myself,
Staring at the shrine of St Ursula, by Memling,
Hanging in the hospital museum at Bruges?
As I am attended by two alien gentlemen,
The saint is attended by 10,000 virgins.
Well, if you ask me, 9,999. There's always one.

I'm with the one that strays from martyrdom.
If I must wear red, let it be these stockings
Or this dress that makes me sister to the sun.
Sensible shoes are strictly for spanking.
My slippers were scooped from the Aegean depths.
When I wear them I can walk on the water —
A party piece I perform when I'm pissed.

I call it an act of homage to my immortal lovers
For I am in the business of making men immortal.
Yet they die on me and leave me to my life.
Damn them, I'll live it, and no man will stop me.
As soon stop the moon or the sun being lonely
As leave me weeping for love that is lost.
Love is never lost, but where does it lead you?

To Adam and Eve, at Ghent, the Cathedral,
In Van Eyck's *Adoration of the Mystic Lamb*,
Severed forever from the touch of each other,
Their lost lonely faces begging for apples.
I plucked them from the painting, they lie now in my mirror,
And when I look at myself, I say, Mother, Father,
Yes, the Wyf of Bath's come home to Flanders.

Traveller

in memory of Barbara Hayley

1 *Japan*

I heard the most wonderful story travelling in Japan.
It is quite true that they overwork you,
But they have strange ideas about time.
It took a horse in the Kabuki theatre an hour,
A solid hour to dance the stage, but that horse —
Its ribboned mane so beautifully stitched —
Where was I? The story that will interest you.

By pure accident I met a young woman,
Called McLaughlin. Your part of the country,
Inishowen, isn't that a tribal name?
There she was in Kyoto, their holy city,
More exotic than Knock, I can tell you,
Learning more about ceramics, she was a potter,
And working in a bar as a hostess —

Why do they so adore Western women, Japanese men?
She was quite lovely and told me this story,
Which is where I started. Have more coffee,
There's a good bottle of red wine buried in that press.
Open it, not for me, I'll pretend I'm Norwegian.
In Norway no one drinks and drives, so at dinner
They all bring a bottle to look at — God help us.

I was telling you of this Irishwoman in Japan,
And one day the woman who owned the bar,
Who by all accounts was usually so calm and kimonoed,
She gathered all her girls together and cried.
Not understanding a word, the Irishwoman listened

And though in her experience the Japanese never wept,
She knew this terrible grief was true.

The Japanese woman, the bar owner, they called her
Mother, she also ran a factory.
It employed those Japanese wounded in the war.
And she was crying because the factory was going under,
Bar profits kept it going, profits were failing,
And she could not fail, for she was Japanese.
She had decided to commit hara-kiri. She meant it.

The night of weeping was New Year's Eve.
The girls trooped in line from temple to temple,
Shinto, Buddhist, even the Catholic Church
In Kyoto, lighting candles to save her life.
They succeeded, she lived, and I like
To think of her life as candlelight.
I sometimes think, I cannot fail, I must not.

If I fail what will become of us all?
Take your time, you say. I will, if I may
Take my time to dance the stage like a strange, beautiful horse.
Yes, I liked Japan, even if they overwork you.
They believe the gods are beneath our feet.
This young woman called McLaughlin told me that.
She believed in such gods. So do I.

2 *Caen*

Do you remember a January day in Caen?
My birthday, and I was exhausted,
Having chaired a whole meeting in French?

We found a bar and I drank beer
And toasted our mutual health;
The beer you could buy for my gift —

I dislike birthdays and all they entail.
I was like women at the end of a war,
Tired and happy, at peace, in Caen.

3 *Maynooth*

Being an only child,
How I longed for a sister.
I am so glad I have two daughters.
Sophie and Celia,
How I love their names.
My close friend, Barbara Hardy,
Her name too I love,
Being like my own.
I instinctively trust anyone called Barbara.
That is vanity.
Forgivable vanity. Forgivable.
So much is forgivable.

This is the last day
I will spend on this earth,
This is the last day
I will spend in this college,
Yes, my last day,
Though I don't know it.
I will act as if I do.
I will tell, what?
Tell Maureen, my secretary,
How well she does her work.
Phone Frank and ask how was Brussels?

Did he and Philip behave themselves?
I hope not.
Ask Kevin and Aoife
To come see my new house.
Ask Peter — well named,
That man is a rock —
To do something, anything,
Knowing it will be done,
For into his good hands
I can entrust all things.
All these things I'd do
If I had time, but time is precious.

And life is fleeting as the wind . . . .

There are days,
Yes, days,
I sit staring
At the white walls of my office.
The sun hits the self-same office
At an angle unbecoming to itself.
So one avoids the sun
And prefers to look instead at books,
I must return one borrowed from,
God, I've forgotten who —
I am growing confused
On the last day of my life.
I should ring Marianna
Gourlandris in London.
She would cheer me up
And order me to find
A good three-volume novel
And get back to the eighteenth century
Where I belong.
Oh Marianna, I wish I did.

Then I should die falling from my horse.
A carriage overturned.
But it will be in a car
Where coffee was spilt yesterday.
A riotous chocolate house.
I do not know it is the last day of my life
No more than I can know
That those who found me dying
Will tell what my last words were.
Am I dead? I asked.
I have always kept my manners.
I could see their distress.
I prepared them gently for my dying
By asking, am I dead?
So they could answer, no,
No, you'll be all right.
Kind,
Even though I knew,
They knew,
We all knew.
And I would weep this day
Buckets of tears
To know it is my last on this earth,
In this college,
But I don't know this,
So I'm damned if I'm going to weep.
I will get into my car,
I will drive and that is that.
That is how I want it, so
That is what I'll do.

And life is fleeting as the wind . . . .

Valparaiso

for John and Kaye Fanning

I'll set sail for Valparaiso
And I'll search for Inca gold,
Turning men's heads with my stories
Of the souls they lost and found.

When I come to Valparaiso
I'll philosophise on why
The Incas never bothered
To see with sacred eyes.

If you ask, Why Valparaiso?
I'll explain by telling you
The trades of the great Pacific
Keep the moon from turning blue.

Come with me to Valparaiso,
Come and find your soul long lost,
It sailed west across the oceans,
Atlantic Pacific dust.

Telling lies of Valparaiso
Does a man the world of good,
No such place as Valparaiso,
Spell it for me if you could.

Turn the letters Valparaiso
To oghams of wood and leaves,
Then remember Valparaiso
When you stand by your grave.

The Rockytown Light

for Eilish and Shane

My mother remembers the Rockytown Light.
It shone by magic during our neutral war.
In Dublin they blacked out windows and prayed
That German bombers would not mistake Liverpool
And land frantic fire on innocent homes,
But here in this town we took to the worship
Of light manifested above barren marshland.

I should add the Rockytown always requires
The definite article before that placename,
As if being definite defined its borders
For none could agree just how far it stretched
As you can Conglash, Sorn, and even Aghilly.
So maybe it is a place for miracles
Since nobody knows where it starts or ends.

But was it God-given, the Rockytown Light?
The priest from this parish blessed the crowds
Who flocked to see phosphorescence dance.
That was all it was, but try to convince
Those hellbent on their right to fight
For their faith in the evidence of their eyes.
The war conquers Europe, this town is bedevilled,

For why is it shining, the Rockytown Light?
O Jesus, protect us, they whistle and sing,
Lead us from temptation and phosphorescent dreams,
A sign of the ending, O Jesus, look
Down and stop the strange visions in the Rockytown.
It's only a mirage, it passes the night,
Such things tend to happen from time to time.

But why is it happening, here, at this time?
My mother remembers. Keep your mouth shut.
Say and see nothing, the best way out.
It will be forgotten, it will all go away,
Or pass into memory, rest assured.
Fire is burning the world and his wife,
Its ovens are fuelled by the Rockytown Light.

The Comfort of His Body

The comfort of his body is a pleasure
To behold. We lie in the Regent's Palace
Hotel in Piccadilly. And he heals my sore
Soul. I love to kiss his gentle face.
I watch him in the morning wipe the sweet
Smell of love from that self-same body
Standing at the wash-hand basin. Neat
And full flesh-armoured, in the mood, he
May turn to me, half-sleeping; he says,
Are you sleeping? No, my love, I'm looking
At the glory of your body. I pray
That your kind flesh, your heart, your cock, your wings
Be tender, hard, be mine. Stay, stay mine.
The comfort of his body brings strength of mind.

Gardeners' Question Time

He is taking stones
From his mother's garden
In the Isle of Wight
Where soil is notorious for the stones.
That's how he spent summer.

Since she moved here
To the house in Magdalen Crescent,
42 Magdalen Crescent,
She's waited for her son
To plant the garden, and he,

Dutiful son, will oblige.
So he moves through the garden,
Dressed in shorts, removing stones.
That is the first stage
For planting anything, anything

At all. Tonight as he undresses
I see his body and, gardener,
I'll question that body
If my rose within his rose
Is my lover's soul.

Dutiful, he will oblige
As he moves naked through the bed,
Mothering stone, mothering stones.
That is the first stage
For uprooting, uprooting anything at all.

Lemon Country

for Sheila and Tom

This is lemon country.
A tang of cold soup.
Garlic and tomatoes.
Sugar for sweetness.
The woman of this house,
A wise owl in the barn,
I am known for the sour
Of my infinite sweetness.

This house in lemon country,
It is mine. I own it.
Just outside Winchester.
The cathedral is mine, too.
A woman is buried there
Whose heart was lost and loved.
I know her name when my heart
Hears her heart in the grave.

Jane Austen, you, too, a wise owl.
There are nights the moon
Betrays my love of flight. I fly
To heaven and it rejects me.
I take comfort from the sky.
The sky is like a son to me.
My heart's prized possession.
Play music with my heart. Music —

Sometimes my heart breaks. I say,
Is the food of love all right?
I cooked it myself. I cooked
The town of Winchester, the cathedral
And the grave. Then I lighten up.
That is my forte. I dance on graves

Of days gone by, possessed by
The moon. This is lemon country.

This is where we live.
Sometimes my heart laughs.
Its laughter is lemon country,
Its taste is good soup.
Garlic and tomatoes.
Sugar for sweetness.
I take comfort from the moon,
And the sky is my son.

Three American Dreamers

1 *Mister Parker in New York*

for Thomas

i

When the conversation in that restaurant
Turned like the wheels of a sorrowful clock
To the death of America, of Kennedy,
I spoke about my music lesson and how
I heard the news that November day,
When I was being driven there to practise
Into perfection some piece I've now forgotten.
Beneath my suit, my shirt, my tie,
My soul loves to sing. Gosh, I'm being revealing,
You bring out something I should not admit.

Bewitched by the two beers on top of wine
At dinner, I turn the table into a piano
And my fingers play the memory of my past,
My present, my future, my hopes to put
On paper the melody of my life;
You see, I have a story to tell, I'd rather not,
But these past months I have held my heart,
My broken heart, and you would not think to look
At me or to listen to my many questions
That my heart could break, but it can, honestly.

Bothered by your asking if I've mourned
My father, beautiful in his living, his loss
So terrible, I say the name Papa and finish
The sentence, telling where he came from in Italy,
Where his family came from to America.
In saying the name Papa, my heart hurts.

I've heard that in New York City
There is a fountain-pen hospital where nibs
And jets of ink are mended. I will send my heart
To heal there and write about my father.

Bewildered by the turn this conversation's taken,
From the death of Kennedy to my father,
I'm content to talk till three in the morning,
The sorrowful hour when the body's weakest.
And to hear you say I have brought you joy
Is kind on your part. You're a good fellow.
I'll hail a taxi soon on Lexington Avenue.
I'll curse you in the morning when I'm late for work.
All my life I've tried to be a good man.
Thank you for telling me that is what I am.

ii

I can't phone you, because I'm busy.
The office has been mad here.
Have you heard of a woman called Lizzie?
Lizzie Borden? That's me. Don't sneer.

Some days I could take an axe
And give the phone what it deserves.
If you knew what I paid in tax,
It could shore the Federal Reserves.

It annoys me that you should josh,
Though I hide it, God damn me,
At the way I call out, Gosh!
When the bastards try to slam me.

Let them slam me, what the heck.
I'll take them on, everyone,
And I'll win, me on the make,
You don't know me, I could stun . . . .

No, I'm not a man for fighting.
I suppose that's been my downfall.
I'm much better righting
Wrongs. Superman. Look, I'll call.

iii

This summer I might not find work,
But it would be nice to go to Europe,
In Europe they would look on my face
And know that it is cut from rock;
I am Mr Parker in New York where
I invoke the names of Saints Peter and Thomas
For Peter is the saint of the rock,
Of coal, of fire, and my father forged me
Thus and gave me doubt. Thomas is doubt.
I move between doubt and fire.
Doubt and fire, that is my dowry.
How strange they sound together, dowry
And doubt. How strange my Roman soul worships
At the Episcopalian Church. I love God
But He's unknowable. Me, I know my job,
I work hard, I'm all right at it.
But some nights my life is a temple
With a fountain at the heart of it
That is my healing voice. Those are your words,
Not mine. This summer I might not find work,
But I'll survive. So will you, you'll survive.

2 *The Finnish Maid*

for Ritva Orfanos

When I left my home in that part of Finland,
The winters red and the summer sour,
To come to work as a housemaid in New York,
The grief was not that like a man leaving,
But relief that a daughter was out of their hands.
She had married herself to America.

Imagine me, a country woman, landing here,
A reindeer lost in Central Park,
The address of Finland Hall in my hand,
And the promise to be clean, decent, hard working,
Send money to my family in Finland,
From my new home where I vowed to be happy.

That is my Lutheran training.
We are destined to do as we do,
And not to find God in love
But in love's renunciation.
This I was trained to believe in
And would believe this day

Until I taste the juice of oranges,
Their scent a stain on my spilt soul,
And pancakes made from buckwheat
The poor can buy in any restaurant
On any street in this part of America.
It is a free continent,

A continent where I'd serve beautiful food.
My family in America do not know
How beautifully I cook. Eggs and potatoes,

Milk, no killing, my hair tied
Back in a scarf of my own fashion,
The fashion of women alone.

While I am scrubbing floors, cleaning ovens,
Roasting meat to perfect heat,
I dream of a cool restaurant
Where there is watermelon, apples, oranges,
And the juice of all this fruit fills
My soul with the drunkenness of God.

I praise the God of compromise,
I follow the middle way. Strange for
A Finnish maid, a woman who left
Her home to seek the earth, to give
Advice to her sad family, stranded
In the great city of New York.

Were you lost, I'd come home to you,
Were I deaf, I'd hear your voices,
Were I blind, I'd see your hands
Guiding me to where you lead me,
And were we all lost, deaf and blind,
We would be gluttons for punishment.

I am a glutton for cleanliness.
I work so hard in New York City.
My family brings me to a garden, full of
Red camellias. Strong colours give me strength.
I am a beautiful woman, a maid,
A housemaid, full of family.

I want no husband in Finland Hall.

3 *The Blue Guide to Ireland*

for Shirley Herz

There is no doubt but that it is useful,
The Blue Guide to Ireland,
To identify these stones of sorrow and
Mourning that question the truth
Of whether or not there is reason
To believe in the woods and gardens
Of civilised people who have chosen
To live in this least densely
Populated land. It is a secret never
To be told that they followed
The way here in the wake of magpies
And killed the harmless birds
Who had made this garden, this wood,
Their own. They are not to be blamed
For the massacre of innocents,
Since it was by instinct they revelled
In the journey westward, for all journeys
Are, in a sense, a way of frontiering
West. The lack of density
In population gave them an illusion —
The illusion that life could be
Endlessly propagated, and so they bred,
Bred like rabbits eating green lettuce,
As famished natives turning green
With envy, and envy is emotion
Destroyed entirely. There are ways and means
Of understanding destruction, but I think
It is best understood as
The Blue Guide to Ireland.

If you can picture the scene of sorrow,
Then you can well understand the tears
And tributaries of its rain have
Contributed to the rivers of Ireland,
Rivers that lose their bearings,
Rivers that flood in the summer months,
Swamping houses in history, mourning voices
Denying death and denying life.
They have faith in fruitless labour,
Time and work all undone, until
In a moment of passion, of panic,
They began to believe in God
And His holy mother, His sad father,
St Joseph, who was not really His father:
Not really, that is an expression
The Irish overuse. It is their method
Of conveying madness, and there is
No method in Irish madness,
But they do have a plan of action
That accords with the wildness
Of their landscape. It has weathered
The storms, the violent storms,
And has shown a face to the world,
A beautiful face, I believe,
A face that has earned its reflection,
That is why I like to look at it,
It doesn't tell lies, it has done its task,
It has served its people, it does its job,
The Blue Guide to Ireland.

Green, they call it green, this island,
But it is blue and it resents
The accusation that it should be
A colour at all, and instead wishes
To be purple, triumphant purple,

The colour of victory, of nobility,
And I think how sad are the dreams
Of victory, nobility, to a people
Whose kings sailed the seas
To live as paupers, as if in a dream,
Where purple is not a colour
But a passion, a panic, a means
Of controlling time, for the Irish
Know that time is no more significant
Than the loss of dreams. The loss
Of stories. All stories are dreams,
I shall tell you my favourite.
The Philadelphia Story. A movie,
You might have seen it. Katherine Hepburn,
George Cukor directing. It's my story,
My film. It made people laugh.
I like the sound of people laughing.
It has healed my troubled soul,
And my soul is staging a comeback
To say what it is I like to see.
Look on the landscape that is my life
In the foreign country that is Ireland
Where I am green and I am happy,
I am the blue guide to Ireland.

Two Songs for Peer Gynt

for Thelma Holt

1 *Peer Sees a Shooting Star*

Brother star, greetings from Peer Gynt.
We're light, we dim, we die in darkness.
Is there none out there,
Not one in the whole multitude,
Not one in the pit, none in heaven?
Poor soul, go back to nothing,
Vanish into mist. Earth, full of wonders, forgive
That I tramped your grass in vain.
Sun, full of wonder, you've wasted your light
Touching a house whose owner was never home.
Earth, and Sun, most beautiful,
Why did you shine at my mother's birth?
Spirit mean and nature wasteful,
It is rough to pay for your birth
With the price of your life.
Let me rise to the highest peak.
I want to see the sun rise again.
I want to look on the promised land
Until I am tired. I will see to it
That snow drifts over me. Write above it,
No one lives here. Afterwards — afterwards —
Let life go on its own way.

2 Solveig's Song

My own soft boy, sleep and sleep,
My hand's my eyes to wean and see.

The boy sat on his mother's knee,
The two played through life's long sleep.

The boy drank from his mother's breast,
In life's long sleep, God grant him joy.

The boy did breathe his mother's breath,
Through life's long sleep, my tired boy.

My own soft boy, sleep and sleep,
My hand's my eyes to wean and see.

My hand's my eyes to see and wean,
My own soft boy, sleep and dream.

The Age of Reason

for Elizabeth O'Haire and Marie McDaid

1 *Hurricane Debbie*

We watched the roofs lift. Donal McLoughlin
Was brave. He crossed the bridge, risking slates.
The whole of Pound Lane trembled. The wind was
Orpheus, lamenting a sad marriage,
Consummated in a mirror. The foot-
Ball field was flattened by a wall
That lost its gravity. No Sunday matches
For ages. Hurricane Debbie sure meant business.
Bottles of milk blew from Bridget Pickwick's door.
Their white fired to glass. It broke children's
Fingers. And guilt was blood on their hands.
All this I recall in hurricane haze.
Thirty years ago, or less. My hands still bleed,
The roofs still lift. I lived near the Pound Lane.

2 *The Doherty Sisters*

There's nights I say the name of six sisters.
Sarah, Mamie, Ena, Bridie, Annie
And Kathleen. Their blind brother, Eamonn.
They're next door neighbours to my grandparents.
Why must they haunt me? What rhyme or reason?
No rhyme nor reason, but the knowledge
Of a passing phrase once dropped. They listened
To Granda singing as he worked in the forge.
Better than the wireless, Sarah confessed.
I envy them that music, those shades that Death
Has hammered into shoes, shoes that have legged
It to life elsewhere, if you believe that.
They did, the six sisters, the Dohertys.
Do they still sing together, in the grave?

3 *The Sore Leg*

Beware if your mother has a sore leg.
It means she's pregnant. Your Aunt Cissie makes
Toast in the morning. Not like your mammy's
Toast. She's gone to Carndonagh Hospital.
With a sore leg. Your mother. She comes back
With a baby. For years this boy imagined
Brothers and sisters sprung from women's feet.
But do you know I'm grateful for that?
The Greeks believed the gods gave birth in ways
Mysterious to man. I've no bother with
Mythologies, but being born, that's the riddle.
I myself have refused to answer this one
By repetition, but I do get a sore leg.
Is it a wonder I'm the way I am?

4 Mad

I spoke earlier of Orpheus, lost
In self-love, picturing a dead wife he
Married to discover she was his sister,
For she was, as he was, twinned with death.
No such madness, thank Jesus, struck the Pound Lane,
But what if it did, who would it afflict?

Say nothing about these subjects. Nothing.
Harm can be done by thinking too deeply.
The mad lie in Letterkenny, scaling
Walls to escape, papering the same walls,
Drinking bottles of stout. I blame the paste,
The paint, the paper. They'd drive any man mad.
The smell, the sound, the sight, the taste. Touched, all.

5 *The Fish Supper*

Am I guilty for associating
The body of Christ with fish suppers?
After Corpus Christi processions —
Flower girls scenting the town with petals —
My father would take us all to Centras,
Abandon my mother to us three, talk cars
And football with Phonsie Centra, her face
A revolution. Ma, your anger's lovely,
You have a perfect right, but your revenge,
Wise woman, is sweet and funny. You order
Six fish suppers; we three are let eat one.
Then you order six more which go untouched.
Not a cheep from Da as you leave the shop,
Smiling, pointing, he'll pay for it all.

6 *St Mary's Hall*

It is very dark in cinemas. St
Mary's Hall was no exception. I went
To the toilet. They are waiting. A gang.

I loved the cowboys and the indians.
This day I really was the Lone Ranger,
A masked man. They kicked the shit out of me,

I was that marked man. I did not know it then
I wore the mark-mask. It took twenty years
To remove darkness from my two eyes

And see the light. They're still waiting, the gang.
Their feet, their fists, their spit. Down in Dublin
I found courage to go back to the pictures,

But still St Mary's Hall is in darkness.
Yes, it is very dark in cinemas.

7 The Wardrobe

You should never move a wardrobe
Downstairs or upstairs. Wardrobes can cause wars,
Especially civil wars. Brothers, sisters,
Divide. They blame their mother and father
For buying wardrobes in the damned first place.
Who needs them? Grown men and women weep.
And then it starts to laugh, the wardrobe.

Jesus, you could kill them for that laughing.
In a matter of time they'll be crying.
The wedding clothes, the baby clothes, the First
Communion suit — save us from their stories.
They go on and on. They go on and on.
The age of reason. Being born's the riddle.
If thou shalt not kill, who then shalt thou kiss?

The World Cup

for Packie Bonner and Nora Costigan

I have seen the world.
It is measurable in miles, yards, inches.
It is the view from my father's eye,
A village, say, somewhere in Donegal,
And I have done my best to save it,
Hold it in my hands like the stilling globe,
Touch it tenderly after the save,
And then let it go, after the save,
Leaving it as night leaves the day
Sky in the east, the sun rising.
I have seen the sun and the sky.
They are measurable in miles, yards, inches.
I have seen the world.

The Japanese Ghosts

1 *Kabuki*

for Anna Nyland

My granddaughter in Tokyo, she dreams
I am alive. I thank her memory
But know it is a dream. Still, in her sleep
I can return as perfumed air from earth.
That's how the butterfly returns to beat
Its crazy wings and wake the girl asleep.
Is she asleep? Was it I who dreamt I died
And went away? I'll ask when I see her.

2 *Sengakuji Temple*

for Peter Holmes and Cathy White

i

May the divine wind scatter the dust
In this place of Buddha. Peace and strength
Attend the Temple of Sengakuji.
Time will forget the purple flower
That has no scent, that is simply itself.

ii

Simply itself, that purple flower
Blooming for dear life in the Temple
Of Sengakuji on this island, Japan.
The violent dead, they too forget,
Their passion all played out in the grave.

iii

Burn incense by these graves of samurai,
These loyal sons. Behead the purple flower
Of forgetfulness. Let incense sting the air.
Here orange trees green with flame, their fruit
The peace, the strength of Sengakuji Temple.

iv

This island's fear of fire is my own,
An Irishman in Japan, in Sengakuji Temple.
Bring peace and strength to my island's dead
That time will not forget. Divine wind, scatter
The dust of the living, violent dead.

3 *A Dream of Aberfan*

for Michael Sheen

That September
                I was thirteen and
                              Lost
                                  My mortal innocence.

Mister Quigley
                Who taught us Geography
                                Spoke of Aberfan.

Wales was rich
                In minerals, coal, iron.

Swansea, Cardiff,
                    They were the big towns.

That was it,
                Wales.

A landslide struck the school — Aberfan.

It buried all the children.

A desperate death,
                    Mister Quigley said.

I was older then, than Aberfan's dead.
We were crying for strangers,
                            Aberfan.

What would have become of them?
                            Played rugby,
Acted,
Sung,
Seen all the mines disapppear,
Been fathers and mothers, those daughters and sons?
Buried in all innocence,
                            Aberfan.

The Corncrake

for John McCarthy and Brian Keenan

Somewhere in Fermanagh it still survives
In the gentle grass, the corncrake,
Thrashing through the field as happy as Larry,
Its piteous cry its beautiful song.

One summer we were plagued by a corncrake,
Cracking its lullaby — harsh was the night.
Next door 'Pat the Twin' roared in unison,
The whole of Marion Park cursed the bird.

What would I give to hear its song now?
Value what you have, lest it's lost.
Guardians of the air, birds of the earth,
If there be paradise, they live there.

They have seen the world. This solitary cell.
As they fly, in chains, can you hear
The corncrake surviving, singing in Fermanagh,
Remember me, remember me . . . .

Hanover Place, July Eleventh

Mo grá tú, lá da bhfaca tú

Grey and semi-circular, the quiet Bann
Divides in two pieces the neat town Coleraine.
From the working-class estate across the river,
Come midnight the eleventh of July,
A powerful water music pounds our ears.
Being English, you did not first know why.

Outside the flat the Georgian front
Slowly decays — a tattered shroud for our haunt.
Tonight you laugh at my worried look,
Here inside the refuge of books and papers,
Your piles of *Sunday Times* a standing joke.
But, between us and them, space thin as wafer.

Aliens at home, this is where we live,
Ireland and England with no right to love.
Worn out, Ireland is first to hit the sack.
England smokes too much, taking a last drag.
Colonize this bed, stop time in its tracks,
Wrap my nearness round you like our flag.